SOLAR
ENERGY

by Kate Conley

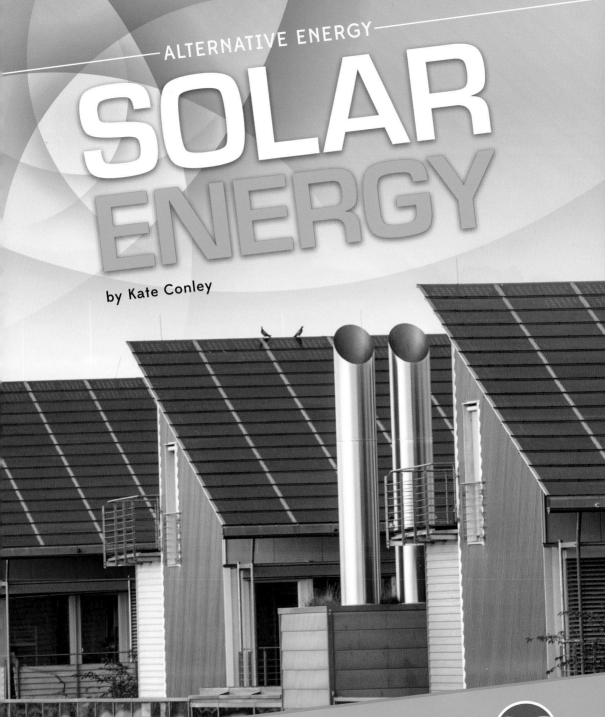

Content Consultant
Hashem Nehrir, PhD
Professor, Electrical & Computer
Engineering Department
Montana State University

Core Library

An Imprint of Abdo Publishing
abdopublishing.com

abdopublishing.com

Published by Abdo Publishing, a division of ABDO, PO Box 398166, Minneapolis, Minnesota 55439. Copyright © 2017 by Abdo Consulting Group, Inc. International copyrights reserved in all countries. No part of this book may be reproduced in any form without written permission from the publisher. Core Library™ is a trademark and logo of Abdo Publishing.

Printed in the United States of America, North Mankato, Minnesota
092016
012017

Cover Photo: Gyuszko Photo/Shutterstock Images
Interior Photos: Gyuszko Photo/Shutterstock Images, 1; USGS/NASA Landsat/Orbital Horizon/ Gallo Images/Getty Images, 4; NASA, 7, 43; National Renewable Energy Laboratory, 8; Shutterstock Images, 12, 30, 32 (middle), 32 (bottom); Adam Hart-Davis/Science Source, 16; Apic/Getty Images, 18; GraphicaArtis/Getty Images, 20; Keystone-France/Gamma-Keystone/ Getty Images, 22; Romas Photo/Shutterstock Images, 24; Patrick Landmann/Science Source, 27 (top), 27 (bottom); Tom Grundy/Shutterstock Images, 32 (top), 45; Markus Gann/Shutterstock Images, 34; Lucarelli Temistocle/Shutterstock Images, 37; Ethan Miller/Getty Images, 39

Editor: Arnold Ringstad
Series Designer: Nikki Farinella

Publisher's Cataloging-in-Publication Data

Names: Conley, Kate, author.
Title: Solar energy / by Kate Conley.
Description: Minneapolis, MN : Abdo Publishing, 2017. | Series: Alternative
    energy | Includes bibliographical references and index.
Identifiers: LCCN 2016945415 | ISBN 9781680784596 (lib. bdg.) |
    ISBN 9781680798449 (ebook)
Subjects: LCSH: Solar energy--Juvenile literature. | Renewable energy
    sources--Juvenile literature.
 Classification: DDC 621.47--dc23
LC record available at http://lccn.loc.gov/2016945415

CONTENTS

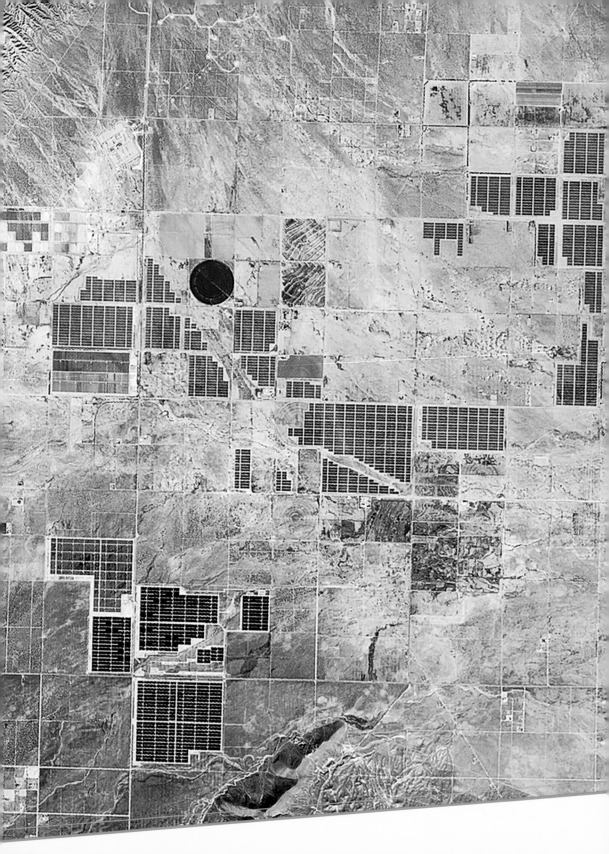

POWER FROM THE SUN

Every spring, orange and yellow poppies bloom in California's Antelope Valley. They grow on land where rattlesnakes and deer roam. Amid this dry, rugged land, 1.7 million dark glass panels sit in neat rows. Each panel turns slowly from east to west. They follow the sun throughout the day.

The valley's panels are part of the Solar Star projects. These two neighboring solar power plants

Satellite photos show the enormous size of the Antelope Valley's solar power plants.

opened in 2015. They are named Solar Star 1 and Solar Star 2. Together, they make up the world's largest solar power station. Their panels turn the sun's energy into 579 megawatts of electricity. This is enough to power more than 255,000 homes.

The Solar Star projects are just two of many new solar plants. Throughout the world, people are looking for new ways to create power. They want clean, quiet, renewable energy. To find this energy, scientists are looking to the sun. It is a power source of the future.

The Sun's Power

The sun has been shining for approximately 4.6 billion years. It is the star at the center of our solar system. The sun is

Megawatts

Solar power is usually measured in megawatts (MW). This is a unit of power. In the United States, solar energy currently has the ability to produce approximately 29,000 MW. That is enough energy to power around 5.7 million US homes. As more cities add solar panels, this number will continue to increase.

The sun's intense energy reaches Earth as light.

made up of burning hydrogen and helium. Its core reaches temperatures of more than 27 million degrees Fahrenheit (15 million °C). The sun's energy travels to Earth as light. Without this energy, life as we know it would be impossible.

The amount of energy the sun gives off is staggering. Just 20 days of the sunlight that hits Earth has as much power as all the planet's fossil fuels combined. But harnessing this power is difficult. Today's solar panels capture only a small portion of it. Still, this small portion is useful. It can power devices and heat or cool homes. It can also be stored in batteries to use later.

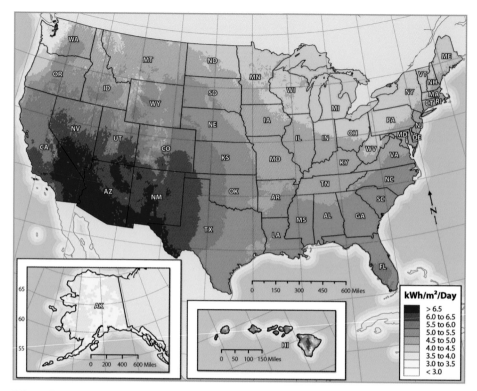

The Sun's Strength

The sun shines on the whole planet, but some places receive more of its energy than others. This map from the National Renewable Energy Laboratory shows how much solar energy the United States receives on average in different locations. The map shows kilowatt hours per square meter (kWh/m²) per day. A kilowatt hour per square meter is equal to one kilowatt worth of energy hitting one square meter of the planet's surface for one hour. How does this map help you understand solar power? What does the map say about where solar power plants might be most effective?

Benefits of Solar Power

Demand for solar energy is growing. People like solar

energy because it is clean. Other sources of energy,

such as fossil fuels, release carbon dioxide. This gas traps heat in the atmosphere, warming the planet. Solar power generates electricity without releasing harmful gases.

Demand for solar power is also high because it is renewable. People can take energy from the sun without fear of using it all. Fossil fuels are different. They are nonrenewable resources. Once Earth's fossil fuels are used up, they cannot be replaced for millions of years.

Sunlight has other benefits too. No company or nation can own the sun. It is a resource all people can share. Unlike oil and gas, which need to be transported, solar power can be used where it is created.

The Drawbacks

Despite the many benefits of solar power, it has seen relatively little use. One reason is that solar power is costly. Solar power plants require many expensive solar panels.

Weather and nighttime are other problems for solar power. Little solar power can be made on cloudy days. At night, it cannot be made at all. Yet many people need electricity at this time. They light homes, cook food, and power electronics. Storing and using solar power at night requires batteries.

A Solar City

When R. Rex Parris became mayor of Lancaster, California, he had a goal. He wanted to make the city the solar capital "of the universe." Parris and the citizens of Lancaster have made great strides toward this goal. Solar energy has become part of daily life there. Churches, schools, office buildings, and car dealerships have solar panels on their roofs. All new homes must have solar panels.

Looking Ahead

Solar power is still a developing idea. In 2015 it generated less than 1 percent of the electricity used in the United States. Many leaders want this number to rise. It is not just a trend in North America. Across Europe, Asia, and Latin America, solar plants are gaining more attention.

As a result, governments are encouraging the use of solar power. The US government has invested millions of dollars in solar projects across 11 states to generate power more efficiently. Some cities, such as Lancaster, California, are even requiring all new homes to have solar panels on them.

With support like this, solar power is no longer just a good idea. It is a reality. People have the technology, skill, and desire to power the world with sunlight. If solar is the energy of the future, the future is now.

EXPLORE ONLINE

Chapter One talks about the use of solar power in the United States. Watch the video at the link below to discover more ways that Californians are using solar power. What new information did you learn from the video?

Energy Literacy

mycorelibrary.com/solar-energy

CHAPTER TWO

THE HISTORY OF SOLAR POWER

Humans have used the sun's power for thousands of years. Approximately 4,000 years ago, people in China started to track the sun. They built homes that faced south. This allowed the sun to heat the homes in the winter. To prevent homes from getting too hot in the summer, the homes had wide eaves. They cast long shadows when the sun was overhead. This kept homes cool.

Since ancient times, people have found ways to use the energy given off by the sun.

The ancient Greeks used similar ideas. In approximately 432 BCE, Greek builders planned a neighborhood in the city of Olynthus. The main streets ran in straight lines from east to west. This allowed all homes to face south. Adobe walls absorbed the sun's heat during the day. At night, these materials released the stored heat. This warmed the homes.

Like the Greeks and the Chinese, the Romans built their homes facing south. They also added a new room called the *heliocaminus*, or "solar furnace." This room faced south and had windows. The windows trapped the sun's heat and warmed the homes.

Burning Mirrors

Ancient people used curved mirrors to start fires from the sun. Burning mirrors focused sunlight onto one spot. It could then be aimed at wood, grass, or dried leaves. The focused rays heated the materials until they caught fire.

Interest Continues

The sun's power has captured the imaginations of scholars throughout history. They have experimented with its uses. In the 1500s, Leonardo da Vinci drew plans for a curved mirror 4 miles (6 km) long. He believed it could be used to heat factories. Other inventors tried to create weapons to harness the sun's power.

Farmers, too, used solar power. In the late 1500s, they began to build greenhouses. These buildings had sloped walls made of glass. This trapped the sun's heat in the building. The warmth allowed plants to grow in winter.

Uses of solar power continued to expand. In the 1700s, scientists began to create solar ovens. They also tried to use sunlight to power engines. None of the inventions had much success. They were not efficient enough to work well.

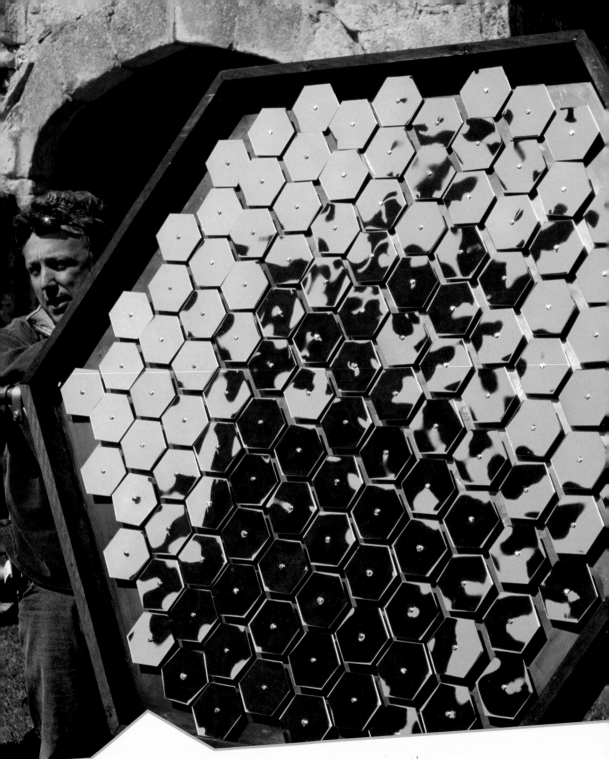

Modern engineers have tried to recreate the sun-focusing weapons said to have been developed by earlier inventors.

A Breakthrough

In 1839 French scientist Antoine-César Becquerel made an important breakthrough in solar power. He was experimenting with electrodes in a special solution. Becquerel realized that when sunlight hit an electrode, it sparked electricity. He had discovered the photovoltaic (PV) effect.

The PV effect is a process that results in electricity. Electricity will continue to be produced as long as the sun shines. Once the sunlight is removed, no more electricity is created.

Scientists continued to experiment with the PV effect. In 1876 English professor William Grylls Adams and his student Richard Evans made a discovery. They were experimenting with the element selenium. Adams and Evans discovered selenium produces electricity when exposed to sunlight.

Adams and Evans used their findings to build a solar tower. They used mirrors and selenium. However, the system was very inefficient. Only 1 to 2 percent

Antoine-César Becquerel was the first in a line of four generations of famous scientists.

of the sunlight that hit the tower became electricity. It would take another century before solar power became useful on a large scale.

A Practical Cell

In 1954 scientists at Bell Laboratories made a breakthrough. They created an efficient solar cell called the Bell Solar Battery. It was made of silicon, a common element in Earth's crust. Scientists added arsenic and boron to the cell. These elements let the cell produce electricity more effectively.

The scientists demonstrated the Bell Solar Battery in April 1954. They powered a model Ferris wheel and a small radio with only sunlight. The solar battery turned 6 percent of the light it received from the sun into electricity. This was much more efficient than older designs.

The solar cells were costly, though. A solar panel that generated 1 watt cost $286. Even small appliances require many watts to run. A radio might need 8 watts. A toaster needs 1,100 watts. To power a home with solar cells in 1956 would have cost approximately $1.4 million. This cost was far too much for average homeowners.

While not practical for homes, solar cells were perfect for the space program. By the 1960s, solar panels powered satellites in space. The solar cells had special advantages in space. They had no moving parts to repair. They also did not require fuel.

The first solar panels were used in a few select industries in the 1950s.

Turning to Solar

In 1973 the United States faced an energy crisis. Nations that shipped oil to the United States began an embargo. The United States lost an important supply of oil. As a result, the cost of gasoline and electricity skyrocketed. Americans looked to renewable sources of energy. One was solar power.

The government funded new projects to make solar power more accessible. Scientists refined the materials and designs of earlier solar panels. Prices slowly dropped. Solar panels started appearing on rooftops. Business leaders planned solar plants to generate electricity on a large scale.

As a result of this work, solar power is a growing source of energy. It is cheaper and more efficient than ever before. More than 1 million US homes had solar panels by 2016. New ones are installed every two minutes. Tax credits and government funding encourage new

President Carter's Solar Array

Jimmy Carter became the US president in 1977. At that time, the nation was still reeling from the oil crisis. One of President Carter's hopes was to make solar power a reality. To show its potential, he had solar panels installed on the White House roof. They were used to heat water for the building.

President Jimmy Carter installed solar panels on the roof of the White House in the late 1970s.

solar power plants. Solar power was once an ancient source of fire and heat. Now it is a major source of electricity for the modern world.

A day after the scientists at Bell Laboratories demonstrated their new solar cell, the *New York Times* sang the cell's praises. The article represented the excitement many people felt over the creation of a new power source:

> *A solar battery, the first of its kind, which converts useful amounts of the sun's radiation directly and efficiently into electricity, has been constructed here by the Bell Telephone Laboratories.*
>
> *The new device is a simple-looking apparatus made of strips of silicon, a principal ingredient of common sand. It may mark the beginning of a new era, leading eventually to the realization of one of mankind's most cherished dreams—the harnessing of the almost limitless energy of the sun for the uses of civilization.*

*Source: "New Battery Taps Sun's Vast Power." New York Times.
New York Times, April 26, 1954. Web. Accessed August 8, 2016.*

Point of View

How does the author of this article view solar power? What does the author predict for the technology's future? Based on what you've read, do you think this prediction has come true?

CHAPTER THREE

SOLAR SCIENCE

Scientists have discovered two main ways to harvest energy from the sun. One way is through solar cells. A second way is through solar thermal collectors. Each method is useful for different things.

Solar Cells

Solar cells are the best-known type of solar power. Most solar cells are made from silicon. This is one of

Solar cells can now be seen in public parks, on the roofs of homes, in solar power plants, and in many other places.

Earth's most abundant elements. It occurs in quartzite rocks and in silica sand. To make a solar cell, workers cut silicon into wafer-thin slices. Each slice may be only 0.01 inches (0.025 cm) thick.

Next, the silicon wafers are treated with chemicals. The chemicals give the silicon an electric charge. Each cell has two layers. One has a positive charge and one has a negative charge. When sunlight hits the two layers, it generates electricity. Thin metal wires in the cell collect the electricity.

To make a cell more efficient, workers add an antireflective coating. Without it, the cell is shiny. Sunlight would reflect off of it. The antireflective coating prevents this from happening. It allows more sunlight to be turned into electricity. Layers of glass cover the cells to protect them.

Panels and Arrays

Joining solar cells creates more electricity. When cells are connected, they form a solar panel. This can also

Top, a worker holds a silicon wafer early in the production process. *Bottom*, a worker holds a photovoltaic cell late in the production process.

be called a module. Panels have many uses. They can power stoplights, street lamps, and crosswalks.

When panels are joined, they form an array. The more panels in an array, the more electricity it produces. Arrays can be quite powerful. They can provide enough electricity to power homes, factories, and even space stations.

Panels and arrays collect direct current (DC) electricity. Most homes cannot use DC. They are wired for alternating current (AC) electricity. For this reason, solar power systems need an inverter. This device changes the electricity from DC to AC. Once this happens, the electricity can be used.

The International Space Station

In 1998 scientists launched the first piece of the International Space Station (ISS). Many more pieces were added over the next several years. Four sets of solar arrays power the space station. Each one has 32,800 solar cells. Scientists can rotate the arrays so they face the sun. Each day, the arrays create between 84 and 120 kilowatts of electricity. That is enough electricity for more than 40 homes. Any unused electricity is stored in batteries. It is used when the station is in Earth's shadow.

Flat Plate Collectors

Thermal collectors are also used to harvest energy from the sun. They use the sun's heat. Flat plate collectors are an example of this type of system. They are often used to heat water for homes or pools. Restaurants, car washes, and other businesses that use lots of hot water also use flat plate collectors.

A flat plate collector is a glass or plastic box with a metal base. It is usually mounted on a building's roof. Water passes through pipes in the box. The sun heats the water in the pipes. Then the water drains into an insulated tank. It keeps the water hot until it is ready to be used.

Thermal collectors can also heat air. To do this, water or another liquid flows through the flat plate collector. The heated liquid then flows into a special coil. A fan blows air past the coil. As the air passes the coil, it heats up. This air can heat a building.

Concentrating Solar Power

Concentrating solar power (CSP) is another form of thermal collector. CSP plants use mirrors to focus the sun's light and create heat. The heat can then

Thermal collectors are often mounted on the roofs of buildings. Each building uses the heat collected by its devices.

be used to create steam. This steam spins a turbine, generating electricity.

One type of CSP is a trough system. It uses curved mirrors to focus sunlight on a glass tube. The tube is filled with oil. The mirrors follow the sun during the day so sunlight always hits the tube. Sunlight heats the oil to 750 degrees Fahrenheit (400°C). The hot oil then heats water until steam forms.

Another type of CSP system is called a power tower. It uses many flat mirrors called heliostats. They focus the sun's energy on a tall tower with a receiver. The receiver is filled with molten salt. It can reach temperatures of 1,050 degrees Fahrenheit (570°C). It is used to heat water to form steam.

Another type of CSP uses mirrors placed on a large dish. A receiver and an engine are mounted at the point where the sun's

Benefits of CSP Plants

CSP plants are efficient. Most of their materials can be reused. The steam is cooled and condensed back into water. It can then be heated again. Likewise, the oil and molten salt used to heat the water can be cooled and used repeatedly.

Another benefit of CSP plants is that oil and molten salt retain their heat. The oil and molten salt can still be used even at night and on cloudy days. They retain enough heat to form the steam and generate electricity no matter the conditions.

trough system

power tower system

dish system

Concentrating Solar Power

CSP systems are promising sources of large-scale power production. They work in many ways. Look at the three types above. What are the similarities and differences?

rays are concentrated. As sunlight hits the receiver, it heats gases in tubes. The gases then power the engine.

No matter the system, CSP plants are usually built on a large scale. They require lots of land and clear, sunny weather. One CSP plant can create approximately 250 megawatts of electricity. This can power 90,000 homes. CSP plants are a promising source of renewable energy for the future.

FURTHER EVIDENCE

Chapter Three discusses many types of solar panel systems. Many people are hopeful that these systems can provide a practical solution to the world's energy problems. However, solar power is a relatively new industry. Many people are skeptical of its benefits. Read the article at the link below. What are the main concerns about solar power? Do you think they offset the benefits?

Is Solar the Solution?
mycorelibrary.com/solar-energy

CHAPTER FOUR

SOLAR POWER'S FUTURE

Solar power has come far in the past 60 years. The first solar cell in 1954 was costly and inefficient. Most Americans were not able to use this technology.

The work of scientists around the world has changed that. Today, solar power is cheaper and more efficient. Vast fields of thermal collectors provide power. Many homes run on electricity from

Solar panels can now be seen on roofs throughout the United States.

rooftop solar panels. Even everyday devices, such as calculators and phone chargers, can run on solar power. It has become one part of the world's solution to its energy needs.

Encouraging Solar Power

Across the globe, governments are encouraging scientists to improve solar power. In August 2015, President Barack Obama signed the Clean Power Plan. It requires 28 percent of US energy to come from renewable sources by 2030. These sources include solar power.

The US government encourages the growth of solar power in many ways. Some programs fund solar panels in poor neighborhoods. Other programs allow people to buy solar electricity from nearby power plants. The increase in solar power creates many jobs. The US Department of Energy hopes to train approximately 75,000 people to work in the solar power industry by 2020.

Jobs in clean energy, including those in solar power, will be an important part of the US economy's future.

Learning from Challenges

Though solar energy is clean, it still impacts the environment. This became clear at the Ivanpah solar plant. It is a power tower in the Mojave Desert. The mirrors used to concentrate the sun's rays create intense heat. Air near the solar towers can reach 1,000 degrees Fahrenheit (540°C). When birds flew through the heat, they died instantly. Approximately 3,500 birds died during the first year the plant was running.

The Grid

When people consider installing a solar system, they must decide if it will be part of the grid. The grid is a network of wires. It delivers electricity from power plants to homes and businesses. Some people choose to be off the grid completely. They draw all their energy from the sun. This works best in areas with many sunny days, such as California. Other people choose to use solar power while still staying on the grid. In this system, owners can sell any extra electricity they generate to power companies. They can buy electricity from the grid when they need more power.

Ivanpah faced other problems, too. After 15 months of operation, it was producing 40 percent less electricity than expected. The boilers required more heat than operators had anticipated. Pipes connected to the boilers leaked. Turbines vibrated dangerously. The area received less sun than predicted.

Solar Goes Global

The problems Ivanpah faces are not unusual. Other new solar power plants have had obstacles too. This is part of

Workers at Ivanpah have faced unexpected challenges, but they hope solving these problems will improve future solar power plants.

learning about a new technology. Many people are still strong supporters of solar power. They hope that as workers gain experience, the plants will run more smoothly in the future.

Nations have put solar power to amazing uses. China is the world's largest user of solar power. The nation is not just creating electricity. More than 30 million solar water heaters sit on top of Chinese homes and apartment buildings.

Solar Products

As solar power advances, people are coming up with lots of new and creative ways to use it. The town of Tenna, Switzerland, has a ski lift with 80 solar panels. It can carry 800 skiers up the mountain each hour. The solar panels tilt to remove snow and follow the sun. In Serbia people can charge their phones at free public solar charging stations. In places where electricity is unreliable, people can use solar suitcases. These small solar boxes can power lights, equipment, and phones at hospitals and clinics.

Germany, too, is recognized as a leader in solar power. In some months, solar power provides as much as 50 percent of the nation's electricity. The United States, in comparison, creates less than 1 percent of its electricity from solar power. This may change soon. As US power plants grow and homeowners install more solar panels, the sun will help power the nation's future.

The future of solar power is uncertain, though most experts agree it has great potential. Stephen Cass of the *MIT Technology Review* explains this potential:

> Of the various next-generation technologies that are considered whenever the future of energy is discussed, cheap solar power is the most promising. Earth is bathed in nearly limitless energy from the sun, and this energy can be used to produce electricity without releasing any greenhouse gases. . . . If we develop adequate storage technologies, cheap solar power could become ubiquitous. Covering 1.7 percent of the United States' land area with solar collectors operating at an efficiency of 10 percent would supply three terawatts of power, enough to meet America's energy needs. . . . In fact, the sun delivers more energy to Earth in one hour than humanity consumes over the course of a year, making solar the only renewable energy source that can keep up with global demands.

Source: Stephen Cass. "Solar Power Will Make a Difference—Eventually." MIT Technology Review. MIT, August 18, 2009. Web. Accessed August 8, 2016.

Back It Up

The author of this passage is using evidence to support his point. Write a paragraph describing the point the author is making, and list two or three of the pieces of evidence he uses to back up his argument.

- Solar power is a clean, renewable form of energy.
- Humans have been using energy from the sun for thousands of years. Ancient people used the sun to heat their homes and start fires.
- In 1839 Antoine-César Becquerel discovered the photovoltaic effect. It is a process through which electricity is created using sunlight.
- In 1876 William Grylls Adams and Richard Evans discovered selenium produces electricity when exposed to sunlight.
- Scientists at Bell Laboratories created the first practical solar cell in 1954.
- Solar power is still under development. Less than 1 percent of US electricity comes from solar power.
- Photovoltaic cells convert solar power directly into electricity.